LINEAR DRUM

A METHOD FOR DEVELOPING MUSICAL LINEAR-STYLE DRUM FILLS

BY BLAKE PAULSON

Alfred Music
P.O. Box 10003
Van Nuys, CA 91410-0003
alfred.com

© 2014 Alfred Music
All rights reserved. Printed in USA.

No part of this book shall be reproduced, arranged, adapted, recorded, publicly performed, stored in a retrieval system,
or transmitted by any means without written permission from the publisher. In order to comply with copyright laws, please apply for
such written permission and/or license by contacting the publisher at alfred.com/permissions.

ISBN-10: 1-4706-1669-6
ISBN-13: 978-1-4706-1669-4

Table of Contents

Section 4: Sixteenth-note Examples

Section 5: Eighth-note Triplet Examples

Section 6: Create Your Own Linear Fills

Introduction

Welcome to *Linear Drum Fills,* a book designed to help you grasp the essential skills and ideas necessary for creating and performing musical, interesting, and exciting drum fills in the linear style. What is linear drumming? Linear drumming is a method of playing drum grooves and fills with a single stream of notes between your hands and feet. Because your hands and feet do not play at the same time, you will not play stacked groups of notes. Linear drumming is commonly used in many modern styles of music, with some of the most exciting examples coming from R&B and gospel drummers. Many of the most accomplished drummers use the linear style to create their drum parts and signature sound.

I hope you enjoy this book and have fun improving as a musician.

Video Introduction

If you would like to see my video introduction to this book, including samples of the lessons and the best ways to practice the material, please visit my website, BlakePaulson.com.

Acknowledgements

This book is dedicated to my parents, John and Coreen. Thank you for allowing me to choose an incredibly loud instrument and then encouraging me to practice it. Additionally, thanks for providing me with lessons, which I consider to be the most fun and effective way to learn any instrument, and start a career.

Thanks to my wonderful family: Bridget Kleinberg and her family; Emily & Kevin Donnelly; Steve, Denise, Patrick, and Spencer Cronin & Elizabeth Rossini; Patti, Kent, and Reina Hardy; Ray, Susan, and Duke Paulson; Andrea Paulson-Metzger & Jeff Metzger; and all of my extended family.

Thanks to my teachers for sharing their knowledge: Scott Crosbie, Paul Stueber, Dave DiCenso, Chris Coleman, Stan Freese, and Brian & Jane Grivna.

Thanks to Dave Black and everyone at Alfred Music for helping me share this book with the world.

Thanks to my students for inspiring me to always dive deeper into the limitless subject of music.

Thanks to the talented singers, songwriters, producers, and musicians with whom I work. You continually motivate me to improve.

Photo credits

Cover photo by Ty Watkins.

Interior photos by Michael Maas: pages 7, 8; Sue Bowen: pages 9, 15, 37, 65, 75; and Blake Paulson: page 80.

How to Use This Book

Linear Drum Fills is designed for all drummers. In order to use this book you'll need to have an understanding of how to play the drumset and read drumset notation. You can play each lesson in the order it's presented, or you can work on individual lessons to strengthen specific aspects of linear drumming. For advanced and professional drummers, this material can be studied on your own. For beginning and intermediate drummers, this book should be studied with the help of a private teacher who can demonstrate the lessons and explain how they can be applied in musical situations.

Warm-ups

When practiced regularly, the drills in the warm-ups section will help you gain greater speed and control when performing linear drum fills. Try to play these warm-ups every time you practice.

Lessons

The two lesson sections examine the skills needed to play one-measure linear fills. Within each lesson you will learn (1) how to add an accent note followed by a break in the first half of the measure, and (2) how to end a fill on each note of the second half of the measure.

To get started, turn on your metronome. The tempos you choose for practicing can vary depending on your technical ability. Typical practice tempos for lessons are between 70–150 bpm.

STEP 1: Using your snare and bass drum, play the rhythm as written.

STEP 2: Replace the accent notes (the X's surrounded by a circle) with one of the choices provided in the accent note key. Experiment with different options to see what sounds best.

STEP 3: Orchestrate the remaining hand notes around the drumset. This is your chance to be creative and make the lessons your own. You will notice how the drum, cymbal, rim, etc. you choose for each note greatly affects the sound of the fill. Have fun as you create your own unique fills!

STEP 4: Add thirty-second note (or sixteenth-note triplet) substitutions. This is another great opportunity to be creative with the lessons. To do this, convert any note or notes into a double stroke. This can include bass drum notes as well. When properly executed and combined with Step 3, your fills will become very cool.

STEP 5: Add various types of drum grooves before and after each fill. This will help you get used to playing fills in the context of a song.

Play each lesson until you achieve a consistent and confident muscle-memorized performance. I suggest playing each lesson correctly many times, with variables in steps 3 and 4. Increase the tempo as you get more proficient.

Examples

The two example sections offer complete two-measure linear fills ending on different notes. Compare the examples with the lessons to gain more ideas on how to create your own linear drum fills. Practice the example fills as written. Experiment with different types of grooves during the slash notation leading into each fill. Start around 60–80 bpm and work up from there.

Create Your Own Linear Fills

Upon completion of the first five sections, you will be ready to start creating your own linear drum fills. Use the sixth section, Create Your Own Linear Fills, as a tool to help you write down your new ideas.

Practice and Performance Ideas

- Muscle memory is the key to mastering linear drum fills. Avoid playing overly fast as this will hinder your ability to memorize the fills.

- Sticking patterns are your choice throughout the book. Experiment with different stickings and play what feels natural to you. Some general rules are (1) use alternate sticking and (2) start each group of hand notes with the same hand.

- The lessons are designed for use with a single bass drum. Many lessons will sound great with a double bass drum, but it is best to master the lessons as written and then adapt them to double bass drum.

- The examples are designed for use with a five-piece drumset. If your drumset is smaller or larger, adapt the notation to fit the size of your drum kit.

- Experiment with dynamics. By varying the volume of certain notes, combined with your orchestration choices, you can produce some very funky and unexpected drum fills.

- Pages 36 and 54 introduce foot and vocal ostinatos (repeating patterns) to the lessons you've already learned. Go back and practice each lesson again while adding the foot and vocal rhythms. For the vocal rhythms, count out loud and focus on keeping your drumming smooth and uninterrupted. Practicing these additional skills will help you gain a deeper level of coordination and confidence with your linear fills.

- Convert the sixteenth-note lessons into thirty-second notes, and the eighth-note triplet lessons into sixteenth-note triplets. To make the conversion, cut the tempo in half. For example, if you are practicing a lesson at 120 bpm, the new tempo for doubling the note value will be 60 bpm. Practice the lessons so the accents and endings fall on quarter and eighth notes. The rhythms will translate smoothly and make more musical sense at double speed.

- Mix and match different parts of the lessons and examples to create new linear fills. This can include combining sixteenth- and eighth-note triplet fills within the same phrase.

- Start the lessons and examples on different beats. Starting on subdivisions can produce very interesting results.

Suggested Listening

While using this book you may want to reference performances of the great drummers utilizing linear-style drum fills. An excellent reference for this is YouTube, where you can hear and see many drumset masters at work. Although I am unable to provide direct links, as they change over time, I can provide some of my favorite linear drummers to search for: Chris Coleman, Dave DiCenso, Gorden Campbell, Mike Johnston, Aaron Spears, and Steve Gadd. There are many more players with great linear drumming videos on YouTube. Search them out and take note of how they use linear fills. Gain inspiration from them!

Balance

This book is an important practice tool that highlights several aspects of great drumming. However, there are many additional skills and concepts necessary to be a complete, well-rounded musician. I suggest using this book as part of a balanced practice routine. Also, if at any time your hands or feet become sore or tired from playing these lessons, stop and take a break. Injury from overuse is to be avoided.

Fills and Solos

Once mastered, the lessons in this book will give you the ability to create tremendous new drum parts. You will be able to use these new skills to play unique, flowing drum fills that your band mates and/or producer will notice and appreciate. You will also find it easier to create fluid drum solos that are as interesting and impressive as they are musical. You will be focusing on one of the most fun aspects of drumming—amazing fills!

Once you identify the essential accents in a phrase, you will have the ability to highlight these figures through a linear drum fill. The accents may be derived from the groove, melody line, solo line, bass line, band hits, ending figures, etc. Many types of drum fills are cool, but a flowing, effortless drum fill that underscores key hits makes you and the song sound even better.

Musicality and Creativity

This book gives you a method for creating musical linear drum fills. Linear drumming is a powerful tool that every drummer should utilize. But as with any tool, its power can be rendered lame when used in the wrong way. In this case, performing a barrage of nonstop linear notes can create the effect of a nonmusical, even mechanical performance. It can sound like you are performing a drum exercise, not a musical fill.

How Can You Make Linear Fills Musical?

- Have your fills highlight important rhythms
- End your fills on the correct note
- Allow your fills to breathe by having small breaks within your barrage of notes
- Orchestrate the notes in an interesting way

The lessons and examples in this book follow these guidelines.

Once you have mastered the lessons, your options are limitless. I encourage you to use your new skills to be as creative as possible. Embellish and expand the ideas within this book to create your own musical linear drum fills.

Drum Key

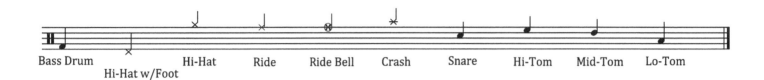

Bass Drum   Hi-Hat w/Foot   Hi-Hat   Ride   Ride Bell   Crash   Snare   Hi-Tom   Mid-Tom   Lo-Tom

Counting Key

Eighth-note triplets and sixteenth notes will be counted as follows throughout the book.

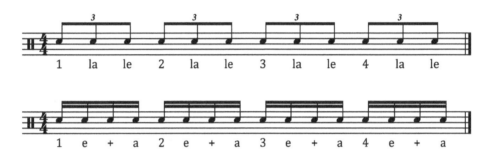

Accent Note Key

This accent note equals any of the following linear/non-linear notes. Try them all with each lesson, and you decide what sounds best.

SECTION 1: WARM-UPS

WARM-UPS
Try multiple stickings for each line.

1. Tempo 90+

2. Tempo 120+

3. Tempo 90+

WARM-UPS

Try multiple stickings for each line.

4. Tempo 120+

5. Tempo 90+

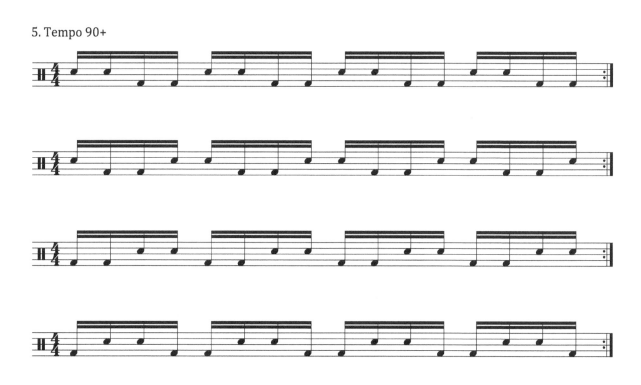

6. Tempo 70+

WARM-UP LICKS: EIGHTH-NOTE TRIPLETS

Try multiple stickings for each line.

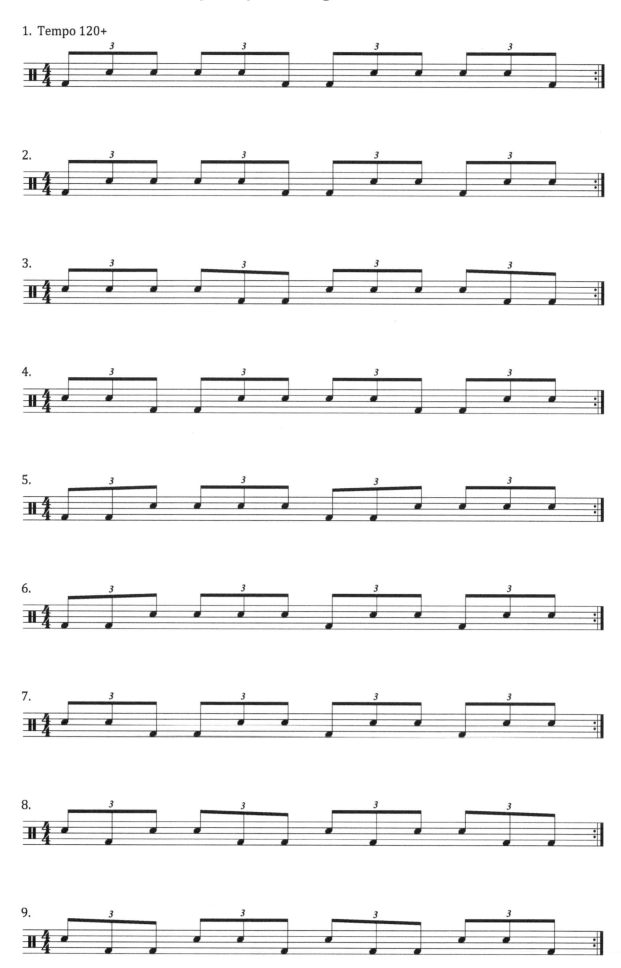

WARM-UP LICKS: SIXTEENTH NOTES

Try multiple stickings for each line.

WARM-UPS: DOUBLE SPEED

Try multiple stickings for each line.

SECTION 2: SIXTEENTH-NOTE LESSONS

LESSON 1

No Break: Hand Lead

1. Resolve to 1

2. End on 4a

3. End on 4+

4. End on 4e

5. End on 4

6. End on 3a

7. End on 3+

8. End on 3e

9. End on 3

LESSON 2

No Break: Foot Lead

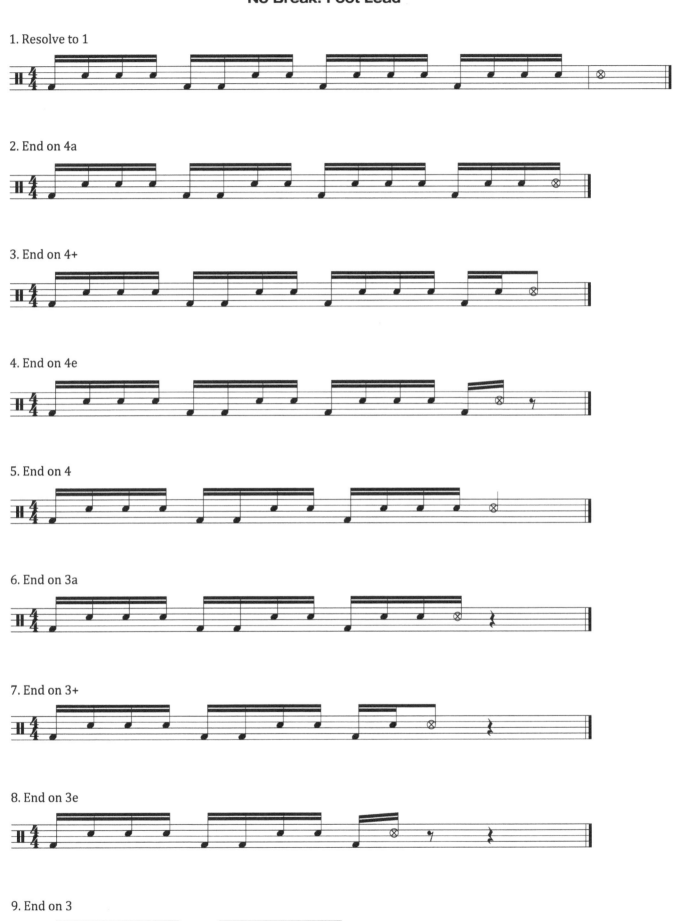

LESSON 3

Break on 1: Hand Lead

1. Resolve to 1

2. End on 4a

3. End on 4+

4. End on 4e

5. End on 4

6. End on 3a

7. End on 3+

8. End on 3e

9. End on 3

LESSON 4

Break on 1: Foot Lead

LESSON 5

Break on 1e: Hand Lead

1. Resolve to 1

2. End on 4a

3. End on 4+

4. End on 4e

5. End on 4

6. End on 3a

7. End on 3+

8. End on 3e

9. End on 3

LESSON 6

Break on 1e: Foot Lead

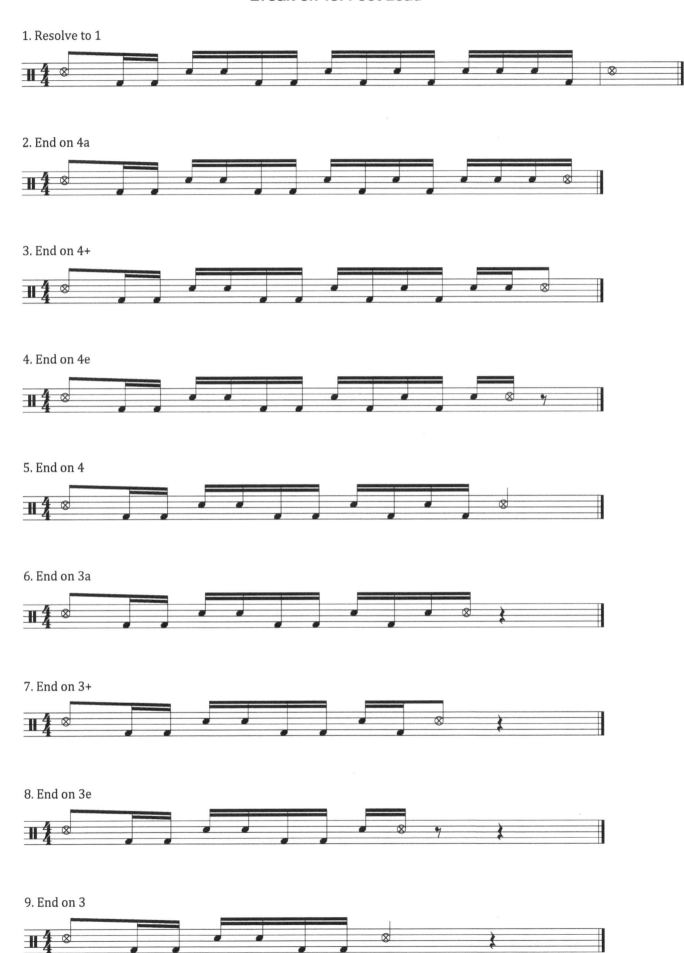

LESSON 7

Break on 1+: Hand Lead

1. Resolve to 1

2. End on 4a

3. End on 4+

4. End on 4e

5. End on 4

6. End on 3a

7. End on 3+

8. End on 3e

9. End on 3

LESSON 8

Break on 1+: Foot Lead

1. Resolve to 1

2. End on 4a

3. End on 4+

4. End on 4e

5. End on 4

6. End on 3a

7. End on 3+

8. End on 3e

9. End on 3

LESSON 9

Break on 1a: Hand Lead

1. Resolve to 1

2. End on 4a

3. End on 4+

4. End on 4e

5. End on 4

6. End on 3a

7. End on 3+

8. End on 3e

9. End on 3

LESSON 10

Break on 1a: Foot Lead

1. Resolve to 1

2. End on 4a

3. End on 4+

4. End on 4e

5. End on 4

6. End on 3a

7. End on 3+

8. End on 3e

9. End on 3

LESSON 11

Break on 2: Hand Lead

1. Resolve to 1

2. End on 4a

3. End on 4+

4. End on 4e

5. End on 4

6. End on 3a

7. End on 3+

8. End on 3e

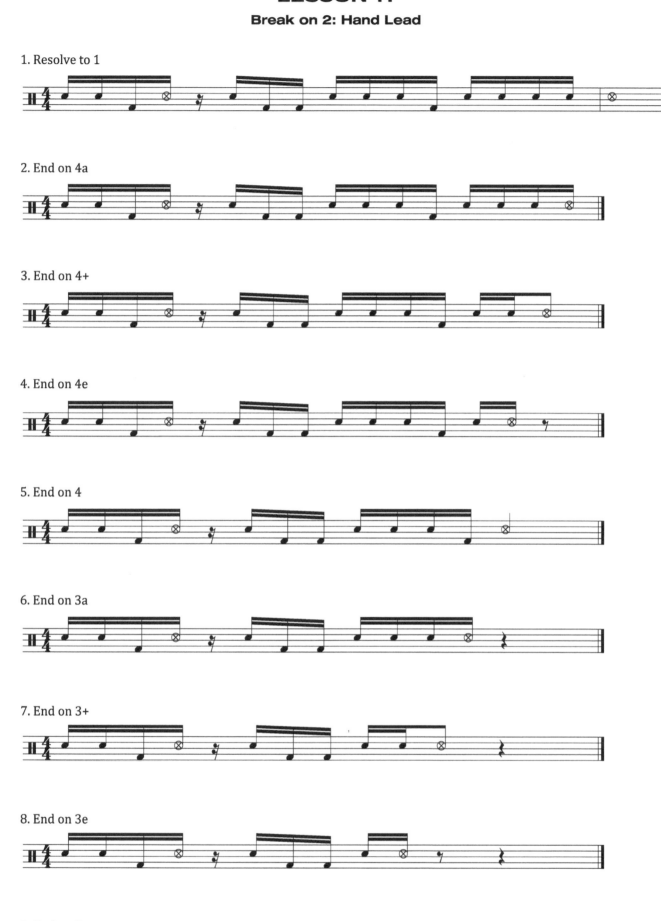

9. End on 3

LESSON 12

Break on 2: Foot Lead

1. Resolve to 1

2. End on 4a

3. End on 4+

4. End on 4e

5. End on 4

6. End on 3a

7. End on 3+

8. End on 3e

9. End on 3

LESSON 13

Break on 2e: Hand Lead

1. Resolve to 1

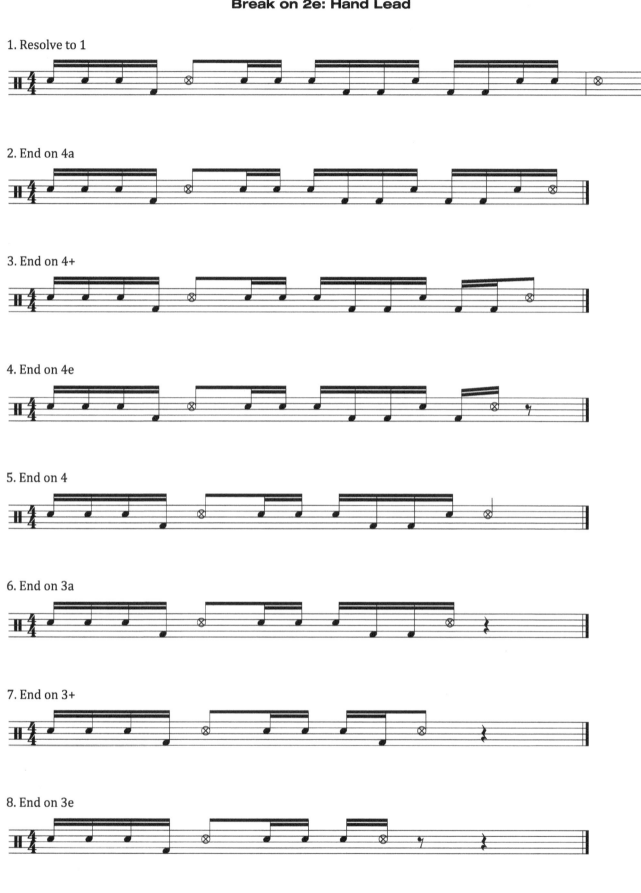

2. End on 4a

3. End on 4+

4. End on 4e

5. End on 4

6. End on 3a

7. End on 3+

8. End on 3e

9. End on 3

LESSON 14

Break on 2e: Foot Lead

1. Resolve to 1

2. End on 4a

3. End on 4+

4. End on 4e

5. End on 4

6. End on 3a

7. End on 3+

8. End on 3e

9. End on 3

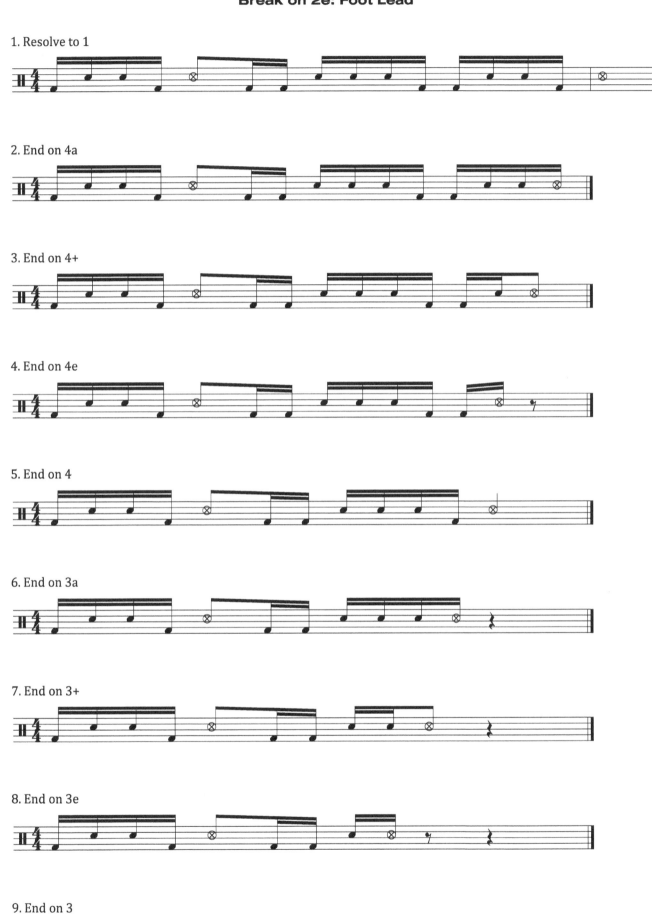

LESSON 15

Break on 2+: Hand Lead

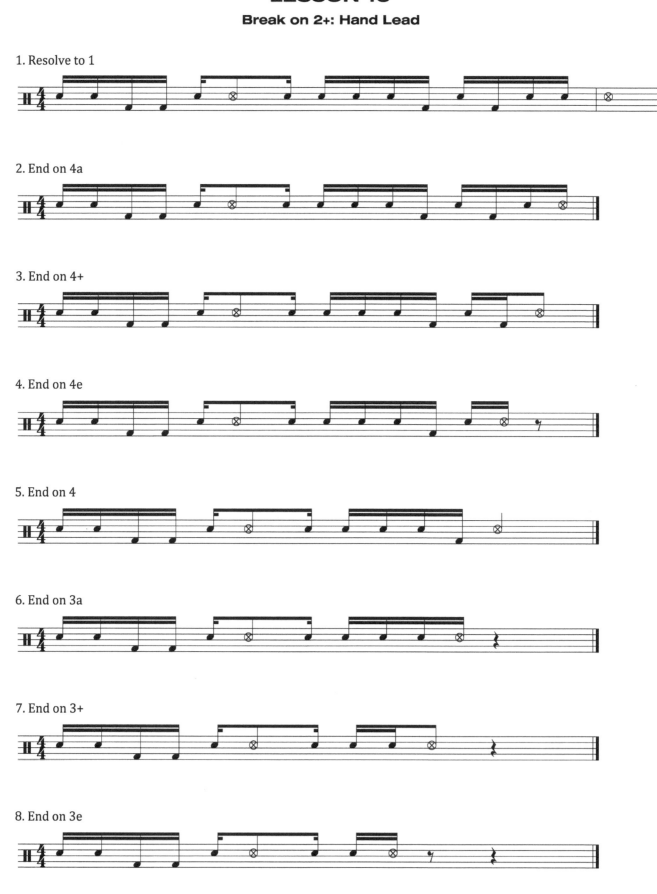

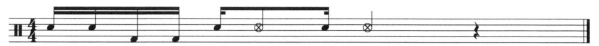

LESSON 16
Break on 2+: Foot Lead

1. Resolve to 1

2. End on 4a

3. End on 4+

4. End on 4e

5. End on 4

6. End on 3a

7. End on 3+

8. End on 3e

9. End on 3

LESSON 17

Break on 2a: Hand Lead

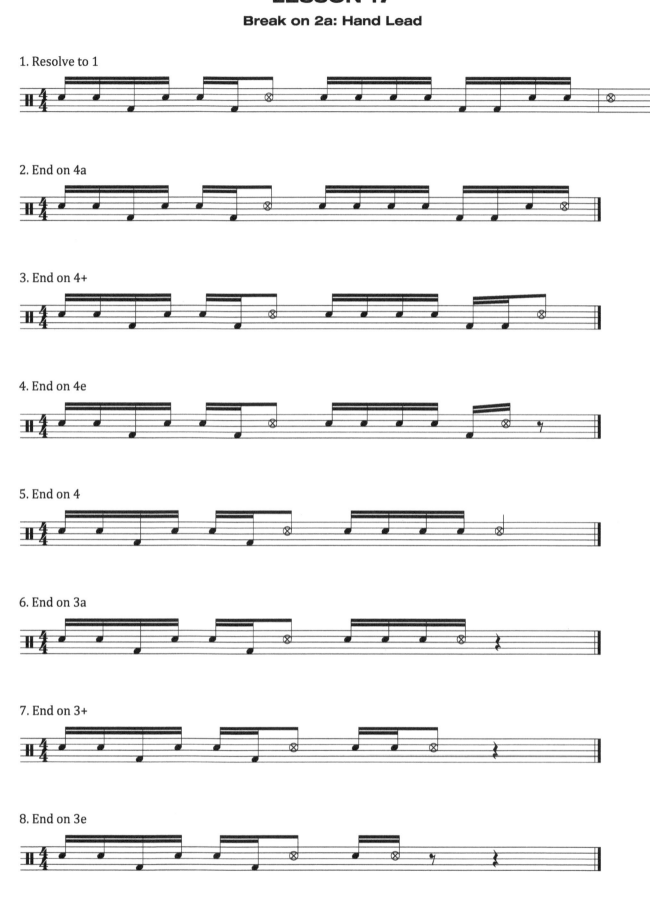

LESSON 18

Break on 2a: Foot Lead

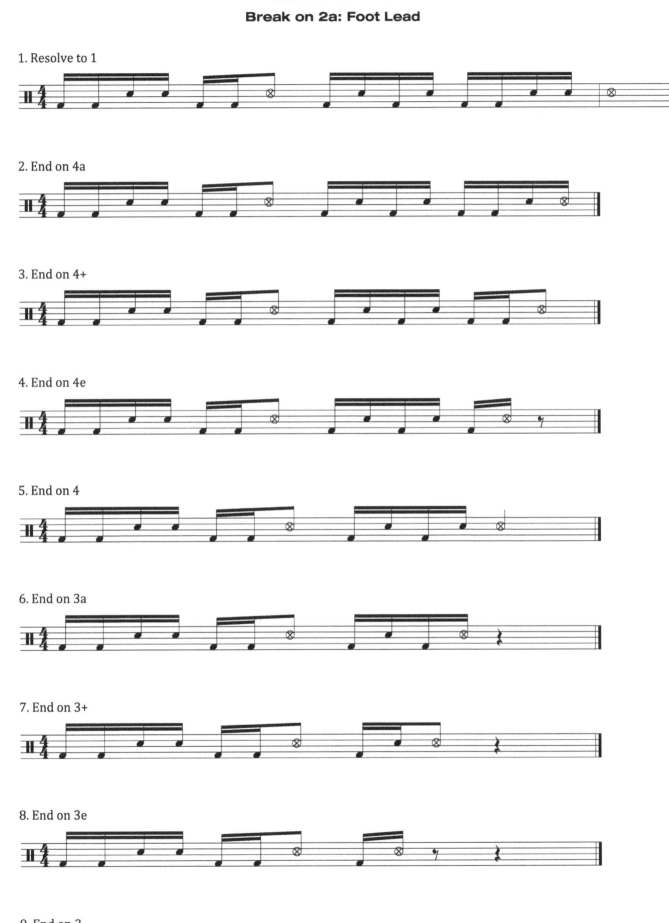

LESSON 19

Break on 3: Hand Lead

1. Resolve to 1

2. End on 4a

3. End on 4+

4. End on 4e

5. End on 4

6. End on 3a

7. End on 3+

8. End on 3e

LESSON 20
Break on 3: Foot Lead

1. Resolve to 1

2. End on 4a

3. End on 4+

4. End on 4e

5. End on 4

6. End on 3a

7. End on 3+

8. End on 3e

HI-HAT FOOT AND VOCAL RHYTHMS
Ostinatos for use with Section 2

Pick a lesson you've completed and play it again, adding one of the following hi-hat foot rhythms.
When finished, pick another hi-hat foot ostinato to try.

Pick a lesson you've completed and play it again, counting one of the following vocal rhythms out loud.
When finished, pick another vocal ostinato to try.

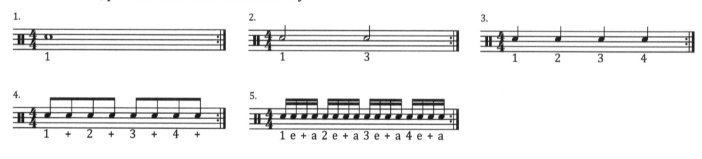

SECTION 3: EIGHTH-NOTE TRIPLET LESSONS

LESSON 21
No Break: Hand Lead

1. Resolve to 1

2. End on 4le

3. End on 4la

4. End on 4

5. End on 3le

6. End on 3la

7. End on 3

LESSON 22
No Break: Foot Lead

1. Resolve to 1

2. End on 4le

3. End on 4la

4. End on 4

5. End on 3le

6. End on 3la

7. End on 3

LESSON 23

Break on 1: Hand Lead

1. Resolve to 1

2. End on 4le

3. End on 4la

4. End on 4

5. End on 3le

6. End on 3la

7. End on 3

LESSON 24
Break on 1: Foot Lead

1. Resolve to 1

2. End on 4le

3. End on 4la

4. End on 4

5. End on 3le

6. End on 3la

7. End on 3

LESSON 25

Break on 1la: Hand Lead

1. Resolve to 1

2. End on 4le

3. End on 4la

4. End on 4

5. End on 3le

6. End on 3la

7. End on 3

LESSON 26

Break on 1la: Foot Lead

1. Resolve to 1

2. End on 4le

3. End on 4la

4. End on 4

5. End on 3le

6. End on 3la

7. End on 3

LESSON 27

Break on 1le: Hand Lead

1. Resolve to 1

2. End on 4le

3. End on 4la

4. End on 4

5. End on 3le

6. End on 3la

7. End on 3

LESSON 28
Break on 1le: Foot Lead

1. Resolve to 1

2. End on 4le

3. End on 4la

4. End on 4

5. End on 3le

6. End on 3la

7. End on 3

LESSON 29

Break on 2: Hand Lead

1. Resolve to 1

2. End on 4le

3. End on 4la

4. End on 4

5. End on 3le

6. End on 3la

7. End on 3

LESSON 30
Break on 2: Foot Lead

1. Resolve to 1

2. End on 4le

3. End on 4la

4. End on 4

5. End on 3le

6. End on 3la

7. End on 3

LESSON 31

Break on 2la: Hand Lead

1. Resolve to 1

2. End on 4le

3. End on 4la

4. End on 4

5. End on 3le

6. End on 3la

7. End on 3

LESSON 32

Break on 2la: Foot Lead

1. Resolve to 1

2. End on 4le

3. End on 4la

4. End on 4

5. End on 3le

6. End on 3la

7. End on 3

LESSON 33

Break on 2le: Hand Lead

1. Resolve to 1

2. End on 4le

3. End on 4la

4. End on 4

5. End on 3le

6. End on 3la

7. End on 3

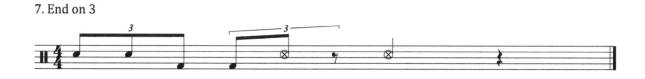

LESSON 34
Break on 2le: Foot Lead

1. Resolve to 1

2. End on 4le

3. End on 4la

4. End on 4

5. End on 3le

6. End on 3la

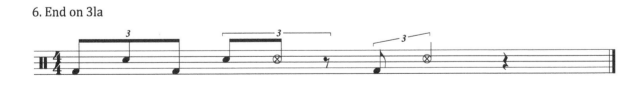

7. End on 3

LESSON 35

Break on 3: Hand Lead

1. Resolve to 1

2. End on 4le

3. End on 4la

4. End on 4

5. End on 3le

6. End on 3la

LESSON 36
Break on 3: Foot Lead

1. Resolve to 1

2. End on 4le

3. End on 4la

4. End on 4

5. End on 3le

6. End on 3la

HI-HAT FOOT AND VOCAL RHYTHMS
Ostinatos for use with Section 3

Pick a lesson you've completed and play it again, adding one of the following hi-hat foot rhythms.
When finished, pick another hi-hat foot ostinato to try.

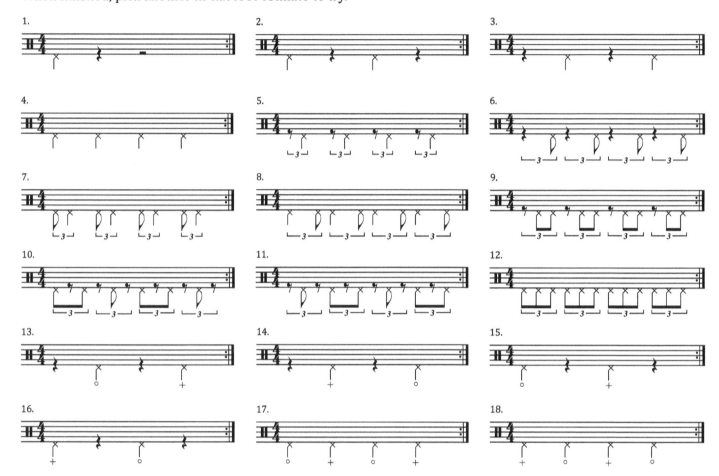

Pick a lesson you've completed and play it again, counting one of the following vocal rhythms out loud.
When finished, pick another vocal ostinato to try.

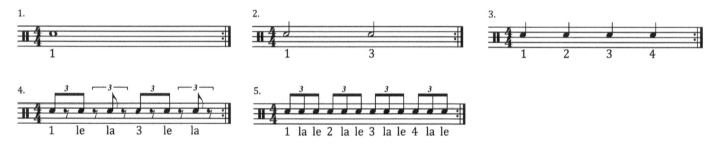

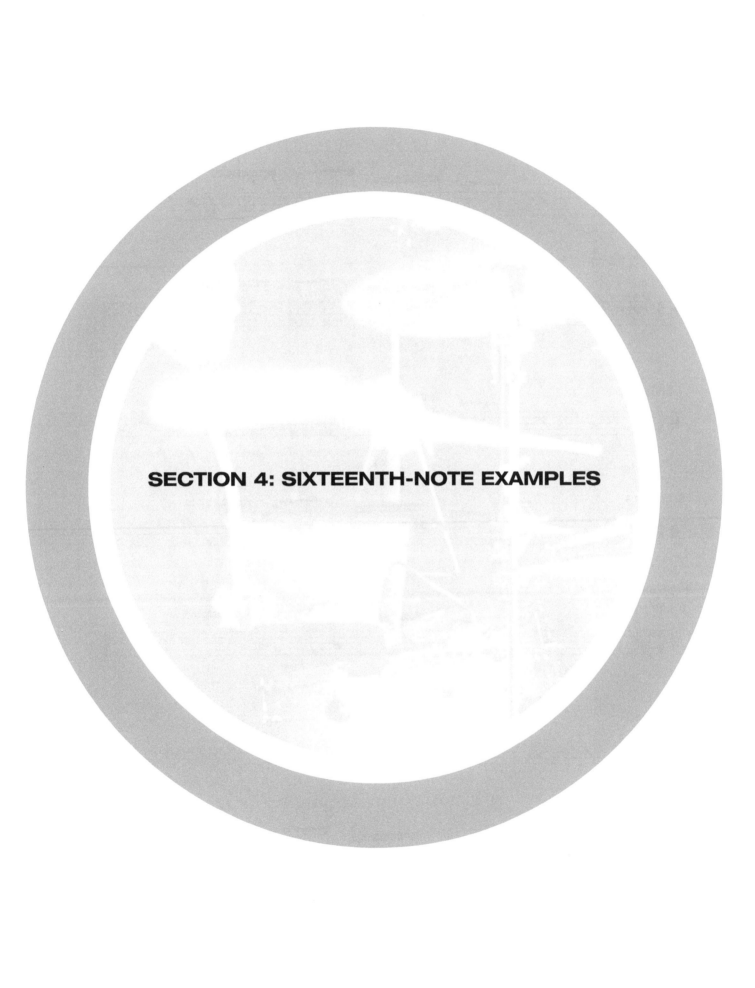

SECTION 4: SIXTEENTH-NOTE EXAMPLES

EXAMPLE A

EXAMPLE B

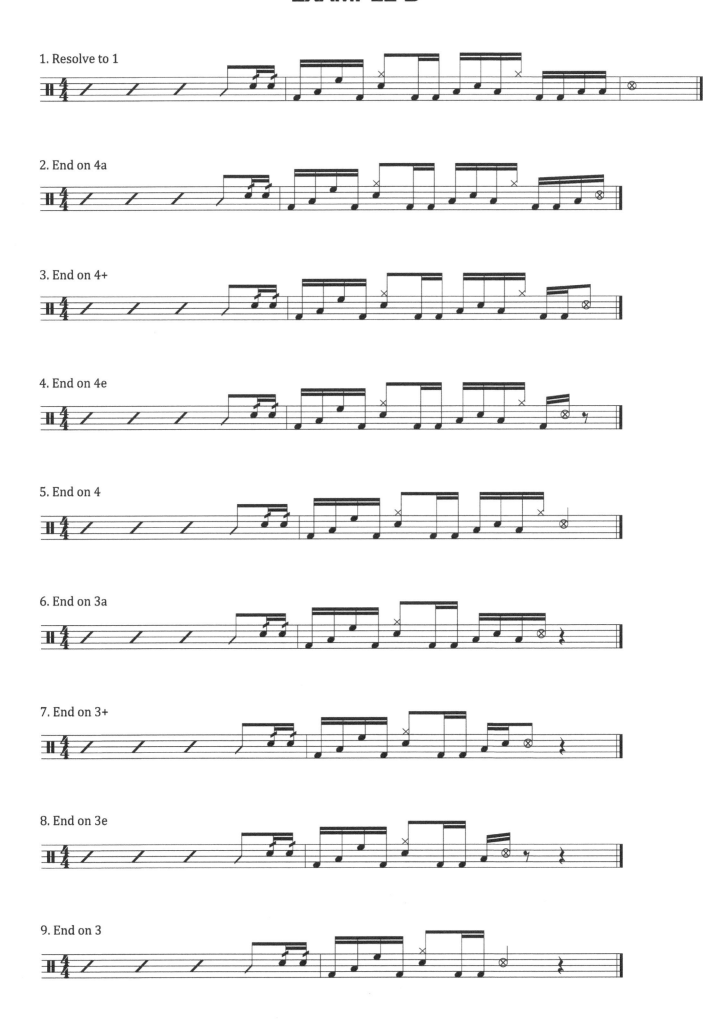

EXAMPLE C

EXAMPLE D

1. Resolve to 1

2. End on 4a

3. End on 4+

4. End on 4e

5. End on 4

6. End on 3a

7. End on 3+

8. End on 3e

9. End on 3

EXAMPLE E

1. Resolve to 1

2. End on 4a

3. End on 4+

4. End on 4e

5. End on 4

6. End on 3a

7. End on 3+

8. End on 3e

9. End on 3

EXAMPLE F

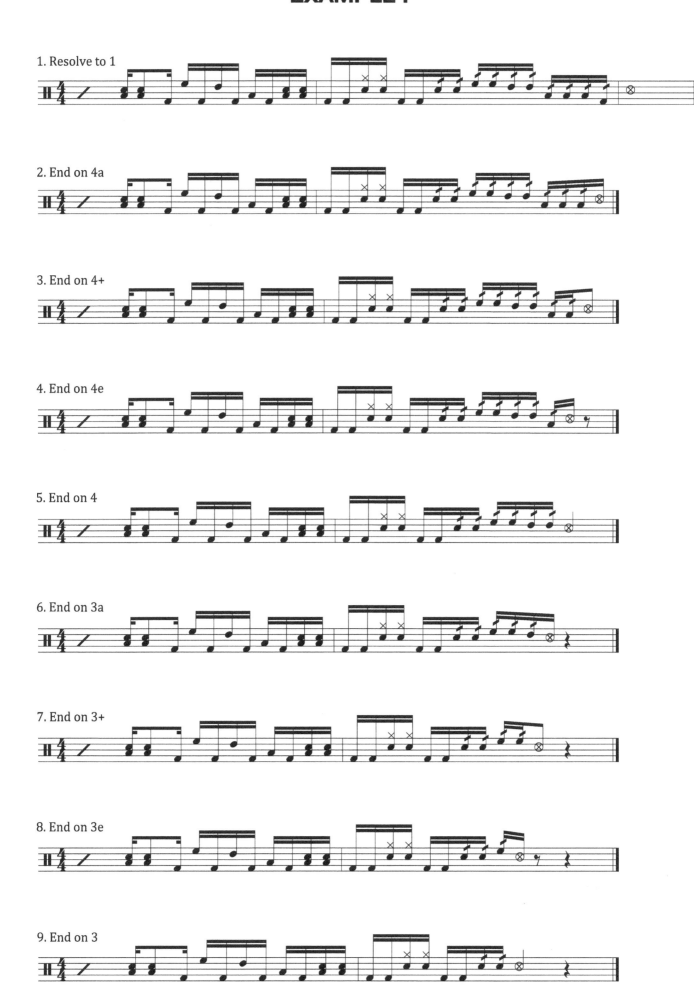

EXAMPLE G

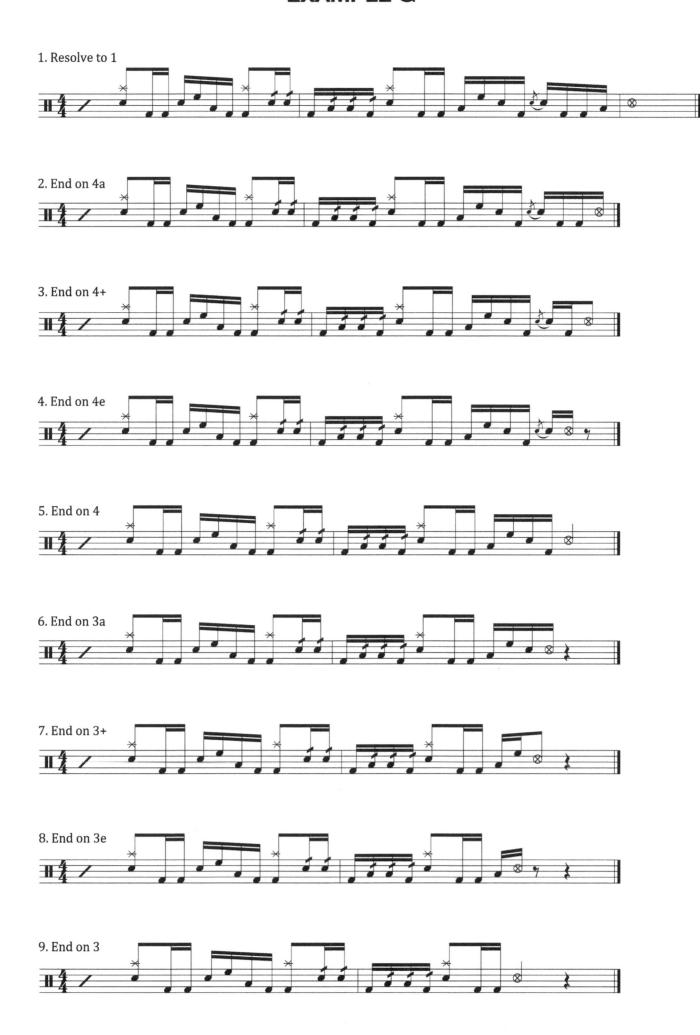

EXAMPLE H

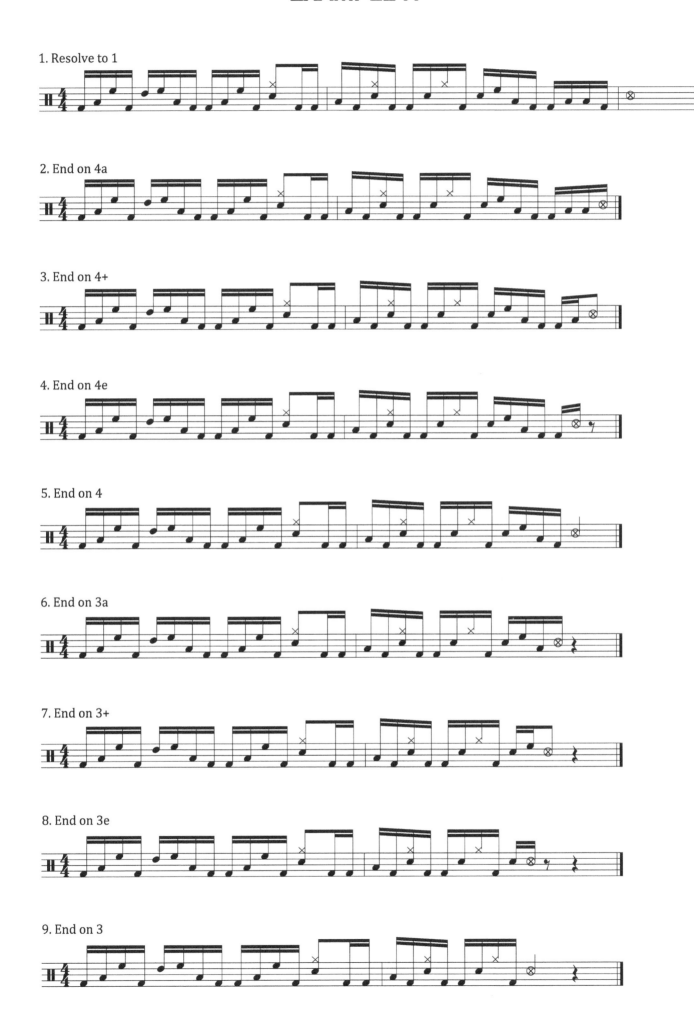

EXAMPLE I

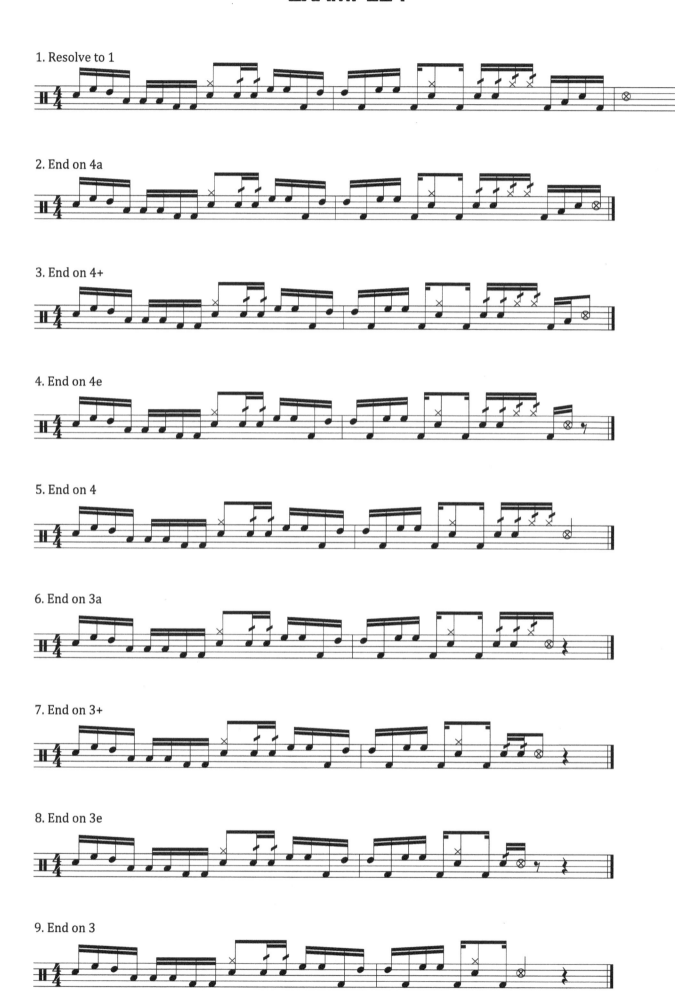

SECTION 5: EIGHTH-NOTE TRIPLET EXAMPLES

EXAMPLE J

1. Resolve to 1

2. End on 4le

3. End on 4la

4. End on 4

5. End on 3le

6. End on 3la

7. End on 3

EXAMPLE K

1. Resolve to 1

2. End on 4le

3. End on 4la

4. End on 4

5. End on 3le

6. End on 3la

7. End on 3

EXAMPLE L

1. Resolve to 1

2. End on 4le

3. End on 4la

4. End on 4

5. End on 3le

6. End on 3la

7. End on 3

EXAMPLE M

1. Resolve to 1

2. End on 4le

3. End on 4la

4. End on 4

5. End on 3le

6. End on 3la

7. End on 3

EXAMPLE N

1. Resolve to 1

2. End on 4le

3. End on 4la

4. End on 4

5. End on 3le

6. End on 3la

7. End on 3

EXAMPLE O

1. Resolve to 1

2. End on 4le

3. End on 4la

4. End on 4

5. End on 3le

6. End on 3la

7. End on 3

EXAMPLE P

1. Resolve to 1

2. End on 4le

3. End on 4la

4. End on 4

5. End on 3le

6. End on 3la

7. End on 3

EXAMPLE Q

1. Resolve to 1

2. End on 4le

3. End on 4la

4. End on 4

5. End on 3le

6. End on 3la

7. End on 3

EXAMPLE R

1. Resolve to 1

2. End on 4le

3. End on 4la

4. End on 4

5. End on 3le

6. End on 3la

7. End on 3

SECTION 6: CREATE YOUR OWN LINEAR FILLS

EIGHTH-NOTE TRIPLETS

Accents:

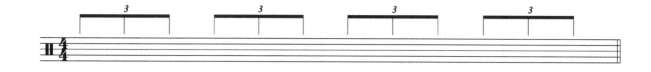

SIXTEENTH NOTES

Accents:

SIXTEENTH-NOTE TRIPLETS

Accents:

THIRTY-SECOND NOTES

Accents:

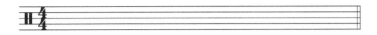

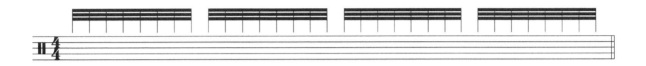

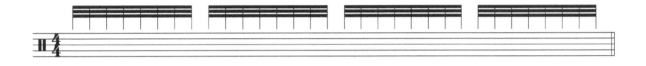

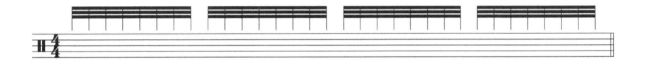

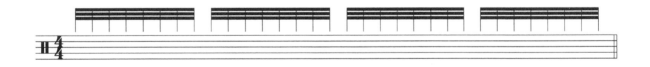

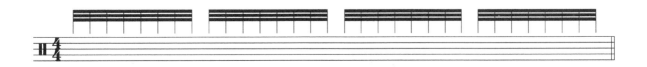

About the Author

Blake Paulson is an American drummer residing in Los Angeles, Calif. An active touring and session drummer, he has worked for many talented independent and major label artists, including Miley Cyrus, Demi Lovato, the Jonas Brothers, and Hoku. He is also a founding member and business director of The Backliners, an L.A. team of session musicians.

Blake's education includes a Bachelor of Arts from Berklee College of Music in Boston, Mass. In 2000 he was awarded the school's Professional Music Achievement Award. Blake's training comes from some of the finest drummers in America including Scott Crosbie, Paul Stueber, Gordy Knudtson, Dave DiCenso, Casey Scheuerell, Zoro, and Chris Coleman.

Active as a professional musician since 1998, Blake has performed across the United States with a wide variety of artists and bands at venues of all types including cafes, clubs, casinos, fairs, festivals, stadiums, and television. His drumming covers a wide range of contemporary music styles including rock, pop, R&B, funk, Latin, jazz, singer/songwriter, and country.

An active teacher and advocate for high-quality music education, Blake has been teaching drum lessons since 2000. He currently teaches private lessons to students of all abilities in Los Angeles.

Blake is also the author of *Drumset Coordination,* a method for developing complete independence; *Drumset Overlay*, a method for developing musical drum fills, solos, and grooves; and *Drumset Supersets*, a combined method for quickly developing speed, endurance, control, coordination, and reading.